IOWA

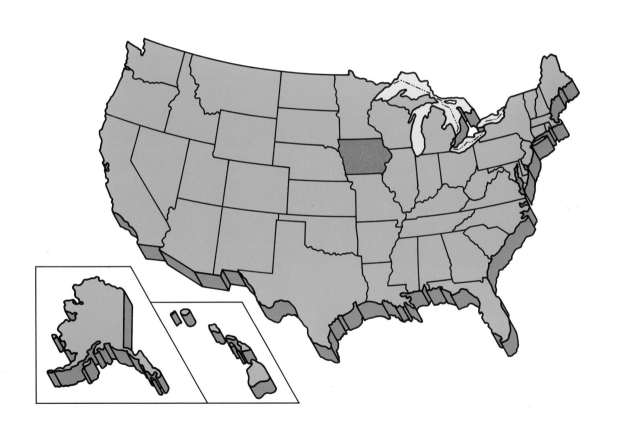

IOWA

Rita C. LaDoux

Lerner Publications Company

This book is available in two editions:
Library binding by Lerner Publications Company
Soft cover by First Avenue Editions, 1997
241 First Avenue North
Minneapolis, MN 55401
ISBN: 0-8225-2724-3 (lib. bdg.)
ISBN: 0-8225-9763-2 (pbk.)

LIBRARY OF CONGRESS
CATALOGING-IN-PUBLICATION DATA
LaDoux, Rita.
    Iowa / Rita C. LaDoux.
      p.   cm. — (Hello USA)
    Includes index.
    Summary: Introduces the geography, history,
economy, people, environmental issues, and in-
teresting sites of the state of Iowa.
    ISBN 0-8225-2724-3 (lib. bdg.)
    1. Iowa—Juvenile literature.
[1. Iowa.] I. Title. II. Series.
F621.3.L3 1992
977.7—dc20   91-20623

Manufactured in the United States of America
2 3 4 5 6 7 8 9 10 – JR – 04 03 02 01 00 99 98 97

Cover photograph by Ty C.
Smedes.

The glossary on page 69 gives
definitions of words shown in
bold type in the text.

 This book is printed
on acid-free, recycla-
ble paper.

CONTENTS

Did You Know . . . ?

☐ Snake Alley, a street on a hillside in Burlington, Iowa, winds back and forth seven times in 275 feet (84 meters). Every May, top cyclists from around the country compete in the Snake Alley Criterium—a bike race up this steep cobblestone street.

☐ The hobo king and queen are crowned each August at the National Hobo Convention in Britt, Iowa. Hoboes hop onto railroad boxcars to ride across the country, and they have gathered in Britt every year since 1900.

Snake Alley

☐ Captain Kirk, a character from the television show "Star Trek," was born in Riverside, Iowa, or so the residents of the town claim. A book about "Star Trek" states that James T. Kirk was born in a

6

small town in Iowa. The people in Riverside decided it was their town, and every March since 1985 they have thrown a birthday party for Captain Kirk.

☐ Sioux City, Iowa, processes more popcorn than any other city in the United States. Each year workers package tons of popcorn and ship it throughout the world.

☐ William Morrison of Des Moines, Iowa, built the first successful car in the United States. On September 4, 1890, Morrison demonstrated his electric car. It sat 12 passengers and traveled at an amazing speed of 20 miles (32 kilometers) per hour!

8

A Trip Around the State

Pick up a handful of Iowa's soil—smell it, feel it, look at it—and you will know that the wealth of this state lies in its rich black dirt. About one-fourth of the best farmland in the United States lies in the state of Iowa. The fertile land produces abundant crops of soybeans, hay, and oats, but the state's most famous crop is corn.

Iowa's landscape was shaped by glaciers.

Iowa is in the heart of the Midwest. Iowa's eastern neighbors are Wisconsin and Illinois. To the west lie Nebraska and South Dakota. Minnesota borders Iowa on the north, and Missouri is Iowa's southern neighbor.

Each of Iowa's three geographical regions—the Till Plains, the Drift Plains, and the Driftless Area—was shaped by **glaciers.** These huge, slow-moving sheets of ice crept down from the north during the last **Ice Age,** which began almost two million years ago. As the glaciers moved over the land, they flattened hills and crushed boulders and rocks.

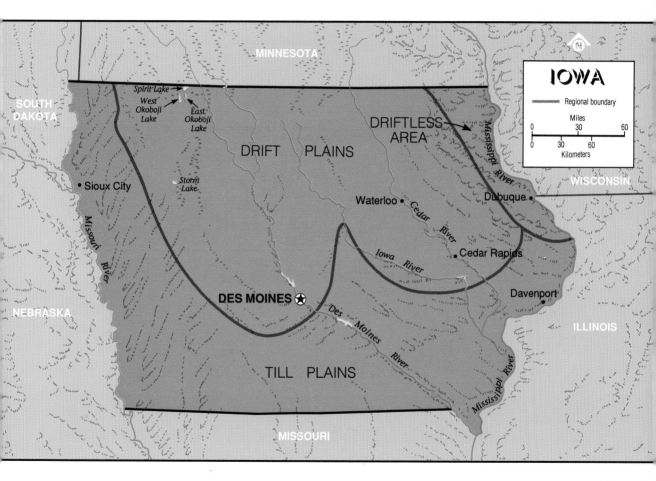

IOWA

Regional boundary

Miles
0   30   60

0   30   60
Kilometers

MINNESOTA

SOUTH
DAKOTA

WISCONSIN

NEBRASKA

ILLINOIS

MISSOURI

DRIFTLESS
AREA

DRIFT PLAINS

TILL PLAINS

Spirit Lake

West
Okoboji
Lake

East
Okoboji
Lake

Storm
Lake

• Sioux City

Waterloo •

• Cedar Rapids

Dubuque •

Davenport •

DES MOINES ☆

Missouri River

Mississippi River

Cedar River

Iowa River

Des Moines River

Mississippi River

11

The Cutler-Donahue Covered Bridge, built in 1871, was moved in 1970 to a park in Winterset, Iowa.

EAU CLAIRE DISTRICT LIBRARY

In the southern and western parts of Iowa glaciers crossed the region now called the Till Plains. The glaciers left ground-up boulders and rocks—a mixture known as **till**—on the plains. Streams gradually carved valleys into the till-covered plains. Farmers now raise crops and graze beef cattle on the rich land of this region.

Iowa's richest soil covers the Drift Plains of central Iowa. The water from melting glaciers washed more rocky material onto the till. Thick layers of this mixture, called **drift,** were left on the plains.

The drift was deposited unevenly, leaving many small hollows. Water collected in these hollows and created lakes, such as Spirit, East and West Okoboji, Storm, and Clear. Much of Iowa's corn grows on the Drift Plains.

As the glacier that crossed the Driftless Area—in the northeastern corner of Iowa—began to melt, it covered the area with drift. But wind and water carried away much of it, leaving the region driftless. Although the land is too hilly to grow crops, it has good pasture for dairy cattle.

For centuries the Mississippi River has been a major transportation route.

Two major rivers, the Mississippi to the east and the Missouri to the west, trace two of Iowa's borders. Short rivers flow across western Iowa to join the Missouri River. Longer rivers—including the Des Moines, Iowa, and Cedar—wind across eastern Iowa and empty into the Mississippi River.

Iowa's location gives clues to its weather. The state is far enough north to have plenty of snow and winter temperatures that have dropped as low as –20° F (–29° C). Each winter, Iowans may shovel 22 inches (56 centimeters) or more of snow.

Spring and summer winds carry warm, moist air into Iowa, making these seasons fairly rainy. The summers can be hot! Sometimes the thermometer tops 100° F (38° C) in July and August.

The setting sun *(center)* casts a pink glow in Iowa's evening sky. Colorful flowers, such as the zinnia *(top left)* and the wild rose *(bottom right),* brighten Iowa's landscape.

Snow geese arrive on the banks of the Missouri River in spring.

Long before farmers began to raise crops, Iowa was mostly **prairie,** or grassland. Narrow strips of forest shaded the riverbanks. A variety of trees thrive in Iowa, but there are no large forests. Oak, hickory, walnut, and elm trees grow in river valleys. In the Driftless Area, white pine, balsam firs, and cedar trees blanket the hills.

Thousands of buffalo once lived on Iowa's prairies, but only a few still roam in the state. The most common animals in Iowa include white-tailed deer, rabbits, foxes, squirrels, and raccoon. Pheasant, quail, and partridge nest in grain fields. Each year, thousands of ducks and geese fly through Iowa on their way south for the winter and north for the summer.

A white-tailed deer pauses in the snow.

Iowa's state bird, the eastern goldfinch *(inset),* **is found throughout the state, which was once covered almost entirely with prairie grasses** *(above).*

18

Iowa's Story

The story of Iowa's people began as the last glaciers melted from the prairies. Indian hunters, the first people in the area, may have come to Iowa as long as 20,000 years ago. They hunted mammoths, huge animals that looked like hairy elephants.

The Indians, or Native Americans, also gathered seeds, fruits, and nuts to eat and made clothes from the skin and fur of animals. They lived in caves and in shelters that they could take down and move easily while on a hunt.

The early peoples of Iowa lived close to rivers.

19

Besides hunting, early Native Americans also relied on gathering nuts and berries to eat.

Another group of Indians came to the eastern part of what is now Iowa in about 300 B.C. These people, called mound builders, built large earthen mounds. The Indians buried their dead in some of these mounds and built temples for worship on top of other mounds.

Iowa's mound builders farmed, planting crops such as corn, beans, and squash. No one is sure why these Indians disappeared about 500 years ago. Scientists believe that wars, disease, or a long period of crop failure may explain the mound builders' disappearance.

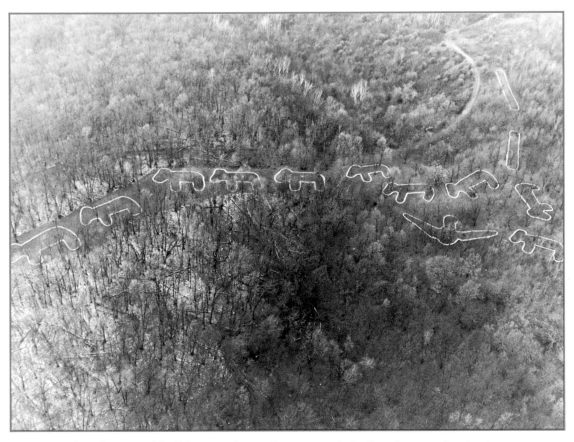

Iowa's mound builders made earthen mounds in the shapes of animals.

The Iowa Indians lived on the western shores of the Mississippi River.

Around A.D. 1500 a group of Native Americans called the Iowa moved southwest into what is now Iowa. The state takes its name from these Indians. *Iowa* probably comes from a word meaning "sleepy ones" in a Native American language.

The Sauk and the Fox hunted on Iowa's prairie.

Many of the Iowa Indians farmed and built villages close to the banks of the Mississippi River. Others continued farther west. Those who went west to the Missouri River eventually split into two tribes—the Missouri and the Oto.

The Iowa, Oto, and Missouri peoples—also known as Prairie Indians—lived in earthen lodges, which they built along the wooded river valleys. In the spring, the Indians planted crops such as corn, beans, squash, and tobacco. When summer came, hunters left their villages to hunt buffalo on the prairies.

Many other Prairie Indians hunted on Iowa's prairies. The Sauk and the Fox, who lived east of the Mississippi River, and the Omaha and the Osage, who lived close to the Missouri River, hunted in Iowa. In the fall, the hunters returned to their villages to harvest the crops and to prepare the buffalo hides.

The first Europeans to visit what would become the state of Iowa were the French explorers Jacques Marquette and Louis Jolliet. In May 1673, they set out to explore the Mississippi River. One month later they pulled their canoes onto the Mississippi's riverbanks in northern Iowa.

Nine years later, in 1682, Sieur de la Salle traveled down the Mississippi River. He claimed the entire Mississippi River valley, including Iowa, for France. La Salle named the land Louisiana, after Louis XIV, the king of France.

Marquette and Jolliet traveled the Mississippi River with the help of Indian guides.

**Julien Dubuque mined
lead near Dubuque.**

During the 1700s, very few white people visited the area that became Iowa. In 1788 the Fox Indians gave permission to French-Canadian pioneer Julien Dubuque to mine lead on their land near what is now the city of Dubuque. Julien Dubuque was Iowa's first white settler.

The region became part of the United States in 1803, when France sold Louisiana to the United States. But most white settlers did not move to what is now Iowa until after the Black Hawk War of 1832. During this short war, U.S. government troops forced Black Hawk—a Sauk Indian leader—and his supporters off their land in the state of Illinois.

After their defeat, the Sauk and the Fox

had to give up even more land along the Mississippi River in what is now Iowa. Many white settlers then began to come to this eastern section of Iowa. As settlers gradually pushed farther into Iowa, the U.S. government forced Indians to sell their land and move west onto **reservations**—areas of land set aside for Native Americans. Between 1824 and 1851, Native Americans lost all their land in Iowa.

Iowa's rich farmland attracted men and women from Ohio, Indiana, Illinois, Wisconsin, and Michigan. Later, people arrived from Germany, Great Britain, Norway, and the Netherlands. Irish miners came to work in the lead mines near Dubuque.

Black Hawk and his followers fought to keep their homeland.

Pioneers built wooden fences around their gardens to keep out animals.

In 1838 Iowa became a territory of the United States. This meant that residents had to follow U.S. laws, but they had fewer rights than people living in states. The Territory of Iowa included the present-day state, most of present-day Minnesota, and parts of what are now North and South Dakota.

In the 1840s, the territory's residents argued about whether or not to become a state. Many people were against statehood. As residents of a state, Iowans would have to pay taxes for the salaries of their local leaders. The territory's residents also couldn't agree on what the state's boundaries should be.

In the mid-1800s, tension was building in the United States over the issue of slavery. Many people in Southern states used slave labor, and slavery was legal in the South. But in the North, slavery was illegal.

In order to avoid conflict between the North and the South,

Iowa's flag has a blue, a white, and a red stripe. These are the colors of both the American and the French flags. France once owned the land out of which the state of Iowa was formed.

the U.S. government tried to keep the number of Southern slave states equal to the number of Northern free states. Iowans were ready for statehood at the same time people in Florida were, so the U.S. government paired Iowa, a free state, with Florida, a slave state. On December 28, 1846, Iowa became the 29th state.

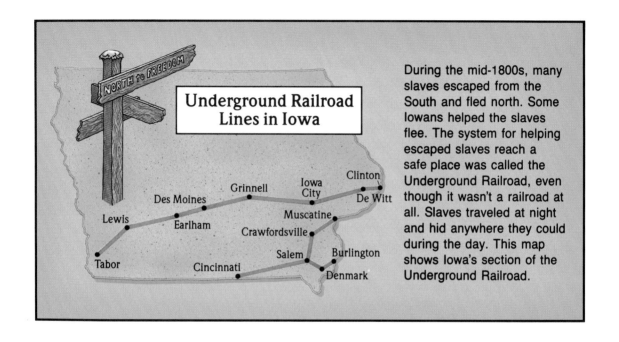

Underground Railroad Lines in Iowa

During the mid-1800s, many slaves escaped from the South and fled north. Some Iowans helped the slaves flee. The system for helping escaped slaves reach a safe place was called the Underground Railroad, even though it wasn't a railroad at all. Slaves traveled at night and hid anywhere they could during the day. This map shows Iowa's section of the Underground Railroad.

The argument over slavery led to the Civil War—the war between the North and the South. The war began in 1861, and Iowa's men joined the Northern forces. No battles were fought in the state, but more than 12,500 of Iowa's soldiers died. Women in Iowa ran the family farm during the war or served the troops as nurses.

Trains were an important form of transportation during the middle and late 1800s.

After the North won the war in 1865, Iowans went to work planting crops and building farms and roads. More than one-tenth of Iowa's land was given to railroad companies. This free land encouraged railroad owners to build tracks in Iowa. Trains brought more people to Iowa and carried goods to and from the state.

31

Steamboat companies competed with the railroads to transport people and goods.

But the railroads charged farmers very high prices to ship their products. Many of Iowa's farmers were angry about these prices. In order to fight the railroad companies, farmers joined the Grange, a national farmers' group organized in 1867.

Members of the Grange, along with many of Iowa's shopkeepers and steamboat owners, urged lawmakers to pass a law that would control the railroad companies. Iowa's steamboat owners had provided transportation on the rivers for many years. The steamboat owners were worried that the railroad companies would take away much of their business.

More people joined the Grange in Iowa than in any other state. In 1874 the first of Iowa's Granger laws was passed. These laws made the railroad companies and the state government work together to set fair prices.

The Right to Vote

Carrie Chapman Catt was born in 1859 and grew up near Charles City, Iowa. After high school, her father said she couldn't go to college, but that didn't stop her. She earned enough money to pay for classes at Iowa State College in Ames. By 1883 she supervised all the schools in Mason City, Iowa.

At that time, it was unusual for a woman to have such an important job. Women weren't even allowed to vote. But Carrie Chapman Catt thought that women were smart enough to make decisions for themselves. So she began to work for the woman suffrage movement—the struggle to give women the right to vote.

In 1892 Catt moved to New York City, where she joined the National American Woman Suffrage Association. She was so good at organizing groups and coming up with new ideas that in 1900, she was chosen to be president of the association.

Catt traveled around the country and was known for her brilliant speeches. To help convince politicians that women should be allowed to vote, she spoke before the U.S. Congress. The hard work paid off. In 1920 the 19th Amendment, giving women the right to vote in all U.S. elections, was added to the U.S. Constitution.

With the arrival of railroads, Iowa's farmers were able to ship their crops quickly to markets in many U.S. cities. During World War I (1914–1918), U.S. crops were needed to feed people in war-torn Europe. Iowa's farmers became rich selling corn for high prices.

To make even more money, many of Iowa's farmers borrowed money from banks to buy bigger farms. But after the war, crop prices fell. Farmers found it hard to pay back their bank loans.

Iowa's farmers sold a lot of corn during World War I.

The Buxton Community

In 1900 a small coal-mining town called Buxton was built in southeastern Iowa. By 1910 Buxton had about 6,000 residents, more than half of them African Americans. Some of Buxton's black citizens had jobs as coal miners, but many others worked as doctors, dentists, lawyers, accountants, teachers, and school principals.

At a time when many public places in the United States were segregated—or separated—by race, the black people and white people of Buxton worked and lived side by side. They went to school together, ate at restaurants together, and drank from the same water fountains.

Buxton didn't live long, though. When the nearby coal mine closed, Buxton's residents left to find jobs in bigger cities. Many African Americans weren't able to find good jobs like they'd had in Buxton. The town of Buxton was abandoned by 1925, but its residents never forgot this early example of equality between black people and white people.

Many of Iowa's farmers did not have electricity in the 1930s.

The farmers' money problems were soon followed by the Great Depression, which began in 1929 and lasted through the 1930s. Banks failed, factories and businesses closed, and workers lost their jobs. Many of Iowa's farmers lost their land.

In the early 1930s, President Franklin D. Roosevelt started the New Deal, a plan to help the nation recover from the depression. New Deal projects helped Iowa's farmers pay back bank loans and buy equipment. Many Iowans were helped when one of the New Deal programs brought electricity to rural areas.

In 1939 World War II broke out in Europe. During the war, most of Iowa's farmers began to plant a new kind of corn called hybrid corn, which had large, high-quality ears. Hybrid corn was so strong that farmers were able to grow more corn than ever before. Iowa's farmers began to make money again because they could sell corn and other crops to Europe for high prices.

By the time the war ended in 1945, many new food-processing and manufacturing plants had come to Iowa's cities. With modern farm machinery to do the work, there were fewer jobs on farms. People began to leave

Researchers in Ames, Iowa, developed hybrid corn during the 1930s.

Iowa's rural areas to find jobs in new factories in the cities. By the 1960s, more Iowans lived in cities than in small towns or on farms.

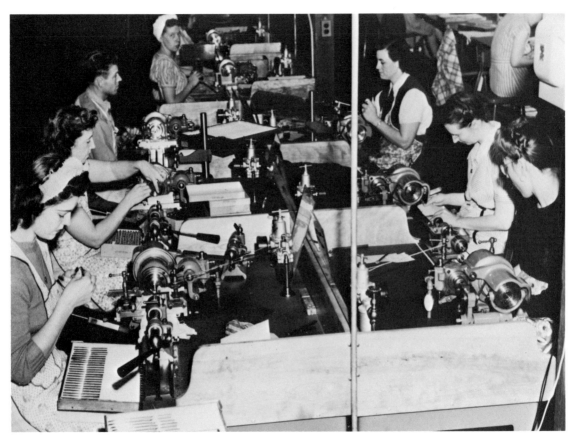

Many women went to work during World War II.

18,000 B.C. 300 B.C. A.D. 1500   1673

Indian hunters follow mammoths into Iowa

Mound builders come to Iowa

Iowa Indians settle in Iowa

Marquette and Jolliet explore Iowa

Iowa's state capitol building is in Des Moines.

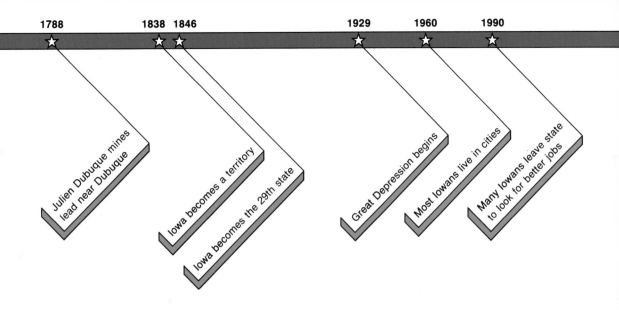

1788	1838	1846	1929	1960	1990

Julien Dubuque mines lead near Dubuque

Iowa becomes a territory

Iowa becomes the 29th state

Great Depression begins

Most Iowans live in cities

Many Iowans leave state to look for better jobs

During the 1970s, manufacturing was earning the state more money than agriculture was. Crop prices crashed in the 1980s, causing more farmers to leave their land. By 1990 many young Iowans had decided to leave the state to look for better jobs. As prices for farm products rise and fall, Iowa's farmers continue to struggle, even though they work some of the world's richest land.

41

Living and Working in Iowa

Iowans are proud of their farming heritage. Most of Iowa's 2,800,000 people have roots on the family farm, although many Iowans now live in cities. Iowa's largest cities include Des Moines—the state capital—Cedar Rapids, Davenport, Sioux City, Waterloo, and Dubuque.

Almost all Iowans were born in the United States and have European ancestors. Some people have African, Hispanic, Asian, or Native American ancestry. About 700 Mesquakie (Fox) and Sauk live on a settlement in Tama.

A young Iowan wears colorful beadwork.

43

Dancing is part of the Mesquakie (Fox) Indian Powwow in Tama.

Iowans celebrate their ethnic heritage at festivals throughout the state. Native American culture is highlighted each year at the Mesquakie Indian Powwow in Tama. Many people dance to German polka bands at Davenport's Deutsche Days. Colorful Norwegian costumes and lively dancing attract many Iowans to Nordic Fest in Decorah.

Each year hundreds of thousands of people gather in Des Moines for another popular event, the Iowa State Fair. Salespeople display the latest farm machines, and farmers show off their best crops and animals. Many people go to the fair to ride the roller coaster or to hear performances by famous musicians.

Music also draws people to the Bix Beiderbecke Memorial Jazz Festival held each July in Davenport. Folk-music fans gather in Burlington each March for the Bluegrass Music Weekend. For people who prefer classical music, Davenport offers the Quad City Mozart Festival in June.

A boy prepares his sheep *(top left)* to be judged at a 4-H show in Des Moines. A musician *(above)* strums his banjo at a jazz festival in Davenport.

Young Iowans of Dutch heritage wear traditional costumes for the Tulip Festival in Orange City.

Many of Iowa's small towns host parades and special events. Each May, the Dutch residents of Orange City and Pella show off their gardening skills at tulip festivals. In June, residents of Corydon act out bank robberies staged by Jesse James and his gang in the 1800s. People in Strawberry Point enjoy strawberries and ice cream as part of their celebration of Strawberry Days each June.

Effigy Mounds National Monument near Marquette features the ancient burial mounds of Iowa's mound builders. Tourists at the Living History Farms in Des Moines can visit a farm like the one their pioneer ancestors might have lived on. West Branch's Herbert Hoover National Historic Site displays the cottage where President Herbert Hoover was born in 1874.

Indianola's hot-air balloon races are popular.

47

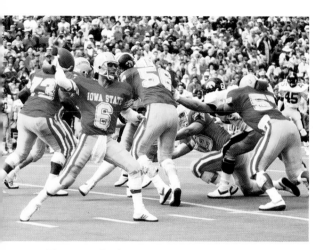

Fans pack the stadium for a Cyclones football game.

Sports fans throughout the state cheer on their favorite high-school and college teams. Wrestling, basketball, track, and softball are popular sports. Nearly everyone chooses sides when the Cyclones from Iowa State University meet

Iowans enjoy hiking through the state's wooded areas.

the Hawkeyes of the University of Iowa on the football field.

Bicycling, golf, hiking, and camping are also popular activities. In the summer, vacationers relax at the lakes near the town of Spirit Lake in northern Iowa. In the winter, cross-country skiers glide along snow-covered trails.

About half of the state's workers have service jobs. Workers in these jobs help other people or businesses. A large number of Iowa's service workers are salespeople. Teachers, doctors, mechanics, bankers, and insurance agents are also service workers. More than 50 insurance companies have their main offices in Des Moines. These companies help pay for damages to people and property.

Des Moines is home to many insurance companies.

Hot dogs are made at this meat-packing plant.

Manufacturing is another important industry in Iowa. Many people make breakfast sausage or can hams in large meat-packing plants. Some Iowans process corn into products such as corn oil and cornstarch. Workers in Sioux City process popcorn. Other Iowans make dairy products. At plants in Davenport, Des Moines, Dubuque, and

Waterloo, workers build farm machinery.

About 9 percent of Iowans work on farms, and more than 90 percent of Iowa's land is farmland. Each year Iowa ranks either first or second in the United States for the amount of corn and soybeans grown. Hay, oats, and alfalfa are also important crops in the state.

51

An Iowa farmer and his son feed the cows.

Farmers in Iowa raise more hogs than farmers in any other state. Other animals raised in Iowa include beef and dairy cattle, turkeys, and chickens. Iowa's farmers also harvest bushels of apples. The red Delicious apple was developed at an orchard near East Peru, Iowa, in the 1880s. The red Delicious is still one of the most popular apples in the United States.

A few Iowans make their living digging limestone, sand and gravel, clay, and gypsum. These minerals are used to make cement and other construction materials. Miners dig coal in central and southern Iowa. Power plants burn coal to generate most of Iowa's electricity.

From farmers to bankers to salesclerks, Iowans depend on the rich soil of their state. Farmers sell their crops and livestock to manufacturers to be processed. Farm earnings are held in banks. And manufacturers and store owners count on farmers to buy equipment, fertilizers, and clothes. In this way, the state's land provides jobs for many people in Iowa.

Protecting the Environment

Rich soil and the promise of abundant crops brought many pioneer farmers to Iowa. Corn grew so well that farmers planted more and more of it. By 1880 Iowa's farmers had planted most of their land with corn. But problems—weeds, insects, and less-fertile soil—eventually began to plague Iowa's farms.

Some plants use up nutrients, or food, in the soil. Other plants fertilize the soil. Corn takes nitrogen, an important nutrient for plants, from the dirt. When Iowa's farmers planted their fields with nothing but corn, it began to use up the soil's nitrogen. In time, the cornfields produced less grain. To produce more grain, farmers spread chemical fertilizers.

Fertilizers add nutrients such as nitrogen to soil and make corn grow better. But when too much fertilizer is applied, the extra nutrients wash into streams and lakes. Then algae, plants that live just under the water's surface, grow very thick.

When the algae die, tiny organisms called bacteria eat the dead algae. With lots of dead algae in a lake, the bacteria multiply quickly and use up the oxygen that fish need to breathe. The fish die or leave the lake.

Farmers also spray their fields with **herbicides** to kill weeds. With its huge fields of corn, Iowa is a breeding ground for insects that attack corn. To kill these insects, farmers spray their crops with **insecticides.**

But herbicides and insecticides can also harm people and animals. When the chemicals wash into rivers and lakes, they can poison the plants and animals that live in or drink the water. Some of the chemicals filter down into **groundwater**—the water beneath the earth's surface—poisoning the water that many Iowans drink.

A plane *(top left)* prepares to spray a cornfield in an effort to stop insects *(top right)* from attacking corn. But too much insecticide can pollute water. So can too much fertilizer, which causes algae *(bottom left)* to take over a lake in Iowa.

57

Planting corn in the same field every year takes valuable nitrogen from the soil.

Because fertilizers, herbicides, and insecticides can be harmful, some of Iowa's farmers are trying to use less of these chemicals. One way to use less fertilizer is to plant different crops from year to year. One year a farmer may plant a field of corn, which robs the soil of nitrogen. But the next year, the farmer will plant soybeans, alfalfa, or clover, which put nitrogen back into the soil.

This **crop rotation** helps keep the soil rich. The farmer will have better crops without using as much fertilizer. Rotating the crops also helps stop the spread of insects that feed on only one type of crop.

Soybeans put nitrogen into the soil, which makes them a good crop to rotate with corn.

59

Instead of spraying an entire field with herbicides and insecticides, a farmer will first check the field for weed or insect problems. If the crops are doing well, the farmer will leave them alone. But if there is a problem, the farmer will spray the section of the field that is suffering.

Weeds can be killed without using any chemicals at all. By using a machine to cultivate, or turn over, the soil between the rows of corn, farmers tear up the weeds the same way a gardener with a hoe does.

To protect the environment, Iowa's farmers are using a variety of methods to take care of their crops. Farmers are working with scientists and the government to find ways to protect the land and its plant and animal life. People in Iowa want to make sure that the rich land of their state will continue to produce healthy crops for their children and grandchildren.

Iowans want to protect their rich soil.

60

Iowa's Famous People

◀ MARY BETH HURT

ACTORS

Mary Beth Hurt (born 1948) followed in the footsteps of her childhood babysitter Jean Seberg, who became an actress. Hurt is a native of Marshalltown, Iowa. Her films include *Interiors* and *The World According to Garp.*

Donna Reed (1921–1986) was born in Denison, Iowa. Reed won an Academy Award in 1953 for her role in the film *From Here to Eternity.* She is best known for the TV program "The Donna Reed Show."

John Wayne (1907–1979), a hero of many western films and war dramas, was born in Winterset, Iowa. He acted in more than 150 films and won an Academy Award for his performance in the 1969 movie *True Grit.*

DONNA REED ▶

◀ JOHN WAYNE

▲ HALSTON

BUSINESS LEADERS

George Gallup (1901–1984) came from Jefferson, Iowa. He developed ways to measure the public's opinion on many issues. The first major success of the Gallup Poll was in 1936, when the poll correctly predicted that Franklin D. Roosevelt would be elected president.

Halston (1932–1990) operated his fashion business from New York City but was born in Des Moines. Halston started his career by designing hats. He branched into clothing design in 1966 and in 1974 was named to the Coty Hall of Fame.

Fred Maytag (1857–1937) grew up in Newton, Iowa. Maytag manufactured farm machinery for many years before he started making and selling washing machines in 1907. By 1925 Maytag's company was the biggest maker of washing machines in the world.

Charles Ringling (1863–1926), born in McGregor, Iowa, formed a little circus with four of his brothers in 1884. At first they traveled by wagon with only two animal performers—a trained horse and a dancing bear. By 1907 the Ringling Brothers had the largest circus in the world.

FRED MAYTAG ▶

▲ CHARLES RINGLING

◀ LEE DE FOREST

INVENTORS

Lee De Forest (1873–1961) began inventing as a boy in Council Bluffs, Iowa. Called the Father of Radio, De Forest received patents for hundreds of his inventions, including the Audion tube, a device for sending radio waves without wires.

Jacob Schick (1877–1937), a Des Moines native, invented the electric razor. His original design was rejected by every manufacturer to which he sent it. The razor was finally introduced to the American public in 1931. By the time of Schick's death, more than 1.8 million of his razors had been sold.

MUSICIANS & ARTISTS

Glenn Miller (1904–1944) was born in Clarinda, Iowa. He led the famous Glenn Miller Orchestra, a dance band, during the late 1930s and early 1940s.

GLENN MILLER ▶

63

Grant Wood (1892–1942) was born near Anamosa, Iowa. Because his high school offered no art classes, Wood pursued training on his own. He became famous for his paintings of life in the Midwest. His best-known work is "American Gothic."

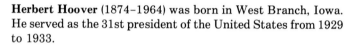

POLITICIANS & LEADERS

Herbert Hoover (1874–1964) was born in West Branch, Iowa. He served as the 31st president of the United States from 1929 to 1933.

John L. Lewis (1880–1969) was born near Lucas, Iowa. After completing seventh grade, he left school to work in a coal mine. In 1935 he founded the Congress for Industrial Organizations (CIO), a powerful group of labor unions. Lewis was also president of the United Mine Workers' Union from 1920 to 1960.

Henry C. Wallace (1866–1924) twice served as the United States secretary of agriculture. His son, Henry A. Wallace, was elected vice president of the United States in 1940.

SPORTS FIGURES

Roger Craig (born 1960) is from Davenport, Iowa. As a running back for the San Francisco 49ers, Craig led his team in rushing from 1985 to 1989. He set an NFL record in 1985, when he gained 1,000 yards receiving and 1,000 yards rushing in a single season. Craig retired from professional football in 1994.

Bob Feller (born 1918) was born in Van Meter, Iowa. He was a pitcher for 18 years with the Cleveland Indians baseball team. During his career, he pitched three no-hitters and led the American League in strikeouts seven times. In 1962 he was elected to the Baseball Hall of Fame.

Janet Guthrie (born 1938), from Iowa City, gave up her career as an aerospace physicist to concentrate on auto racing. In 1977 she was the first woman ever to qualify and drive in the Indianapolis 500. Although her engine failed that year and she could not finish, Guthrie returned in 1978 to become the first woman to complete the race.

▲ BOB FELLER

◀ ANN LANDERS

JANET GUTHRIE ▶

WRITERS & JOURNALISTS

Virginia Allen Jensen (born 1927) comes from Des Moines but lives and works in Copenhagen, Denmark. Jensen is a writer and translator of children's books.

▲ ABIGAIL VAN BUREN

Ann Landers (Esther Pauline Friedman Lederer) and **Abigail Van Buren** (Pauline Esther Friedman Phillips) were born on July 4, 1918, in Sioux City, Iowa. The identical twin sisters have written separate advice columns for more than 40 years.

HARRY REASONER ▶

Harry Reasoner (1923–1991), a native of Dakota City, Iowa, worked in national television news for 35 years. He was a reporter, news correspondent, and anchor for CBS and ABC.

65

Facts-at-a-Glance

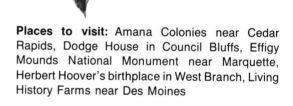

Nickname: Hawkeye State
Song: "The Song of Iowa"
Motto: Our Liberties We Prize and Our Rights
We Will Maintain
Flower: wild rose
Tree: oak
Bird: eastern goldfinch

Population: 2,776,755*
Rank in population, nationwide: 30th
Area: 56,276 sq mi (145,755 sq km)
Rank in area, nationwide: 26th
Date and ranking of statehood:
December 28, 1846, the 29th state
Capital: Des Moines
Major cities (and populations*):
Des Moines (193,187), Cedar Rapids
(108,751), Davenport (95,333), Sioux City
(80,505), Waterloo (66,467)
U.S. senators: 2
U.S. representatives: 6
Electoral votes: 8

*1990 census

Places to visit: Amana Colonies near Cedar
Rapids, Dodge House in Council Bluffs, Effigy
Mounds National Monument near Marquette,
Herbert Hoover's birthplace in West Branch, Living
History Farms near Des Moines

Annual events: Estherville Winter Sports Festival
(Feb.), Grant Wood Art Festival in Stone City (June),
Register's Annual Great Bicycle Ride Across Iowa
(July), National Balloon Classic in Indianola (Aug.),
Covered Bridge Festival in Winterset (Oct.)

66

Natural resources: soil, water, limestone, shale, sand and gravel, clay, coal, gypsum

Agricultural products: corn, soybeans, oats, hay, alfalfa, flaxseed, rye, wheat, apples, hogs, beef cattle, milk, poultry, sheep

Manufactured goods: food products, farm machinery, electrical equipment, chemicals, printed materials, metal products

ENDANGERED SPECIES
Mammals—Indiana bat, Plains pocket mouse, red-backed vole, bobcat
Birds—peregrine falcon, piping plover, common barn owl, bald eagle, king rail, short-eared owl
Fish—pugnose shiner, freckled madtom
Reptiles—yellow mud turtle, Great Plains skink, yellow-bellied water snake
Plants—woodland horsetail, showy lady's slipper, buffalo grass, tumblegrass, bunchberry, water marigold, wild lupine, bogbean, buttonweed

WHERE IOWANS WORK
Services—55 percent
   (services includes jobs in trade; community, social, & personal services; finance, insurance & real estate; transportation, communication, & utilities)
Manufacturing—17 percent
Government—16 percent
Agriculture—9 percent
Construction—3 percent

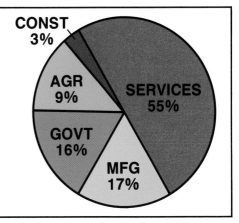

CONST 3%
AGR 9%
SERVICES 55%
GOVT 16%
MFG 17%

PRONUNCIATION GUIDE

Beiderbecke, Bix
(BYD-ur-behk, BIHKS)

Corydon (KAWR-uh-duhn)

Decorah (dih-KOHR-uh)

Des Moines (dih-MOYN)

Dubuque (duh-BYOOK)

Jolliet, Louis
(JOH-lee-eht, LOO-ihs)

La Salle, Sieur de
(luh-SAL, syu duh)

Marquette, Jacques
(mahr-KEHT, ZHAHK)

Mesquakie (muhs-KWAW-kee)

Okoboji (oh-kuh-BOH-jee)

Osage (oh-SAYJ)

Glossary

crop rotation Alternating the crops grown in a field from one year to the next to replace the minerals taken from the soil by one type of crop.

drift A mixture of clay, sand, gravel, and boulders deposited by a glacier, plus any materials added to this mixture by the running water of a melting glacier. Areas where drift has been deposited have very good soil for farming.

glacier A large body of ice and snow that moves slowly over land.

groundwater Water that lies beneath the earth's surface. The water comes from rain and snow that seep through soil into the cracks and other openings in rocks. Groundwater supplies wells and springs.

herbicide Chemicals used to destroy or control the growth of unwanted plants such as weeds.

ice age A period when ice sheets cover large regions of the earth. The term *Ice Age* usually refers to the most recent one, called the Pleistocene, which began almost 2 million years ago and ended about 10,000 years ago.

insecticide A substance that kills insects.

prairie A large area of level or gently rolling grassy land with few trees.

reservation Public land set aside by the government to be used by Native Americans.

till A mixture of clay, sand, gravel, and boulders deposited by a glacier.

Index ▬▬▬▬

71

Acknowledgments:

Maryland Cartographics, Inc., pp. 2, 11; Kent & Donna Dannen, pp. 2–3, 10, 14, 48 (right); Lynda Richards, pp. 6, 12, 15 (top left), 19, 37, 42, 43, 46 (right), 47, 49, 55, 60, 68, 71; Jack Lindstrom, p. 7; James Blank/Root Resources, p. 8; Jeff Greenberg, pp. 9, 35, 57 (top left); Ty C. Smedes, pp. 15 (center), 16, 17, 18 (inset), 20, 61; Lucille Sukalo, p. 15 (bottom right); Colleen Sexton, pp. 18, 59; State Historical Society of Iowa-Iowa City, pp. 21, 22, 26, 39, 64 (center right); State Historical Society of Iowa-Des Moines, pp. 31, 32–33, 34, 36, 44; Independent Picture Service, p. 23, 62 (bottom left); National Archives Canada, Ottawa (C–8486189) detail, p. 25; National Collection of Fine Arts, Smithsonian Institution, p. 27; Kay Shaw Photography, pp. 28, 38, 45 (left), 53; Root Resources, p. 41; Quad Cities CVB/Basil Williams, p. 45 (right); Orange City Chamber & Tulip Festival Steering Commerce, p. 46 (left); Iowa State University News Service, Photo Dept., Ames, Iowa, 50011, p. 48 (left); Oscar Mayer Foods Corporation, p. 50; JOLLY TIME Pop Corn, pp. 51, 58; USDA-Soil Conservation Service, p. 57 (bottom left); Ken Ostlie/University of Minnesota-Department of Entomology, p. 57 (top right); Hollywood Book & Poster Co., p. 62 (top right and left), p. 63 (bottom); Halston for Men, p. 62 (bottom right); Maytag Company, p. 63 (top left); Circus World Museum, Baraboo, Wisconsin, p. 63 (top right); Library of Congress, p. 63 (center), p. 64 (top right); The George Meany Memorial Archives, p. 64 (center left); San Francisco 49ers, p. 64 (bottom); © Indy 500 Photos, p. 65 (top left); Stew Thornley, p. 65 (top right); AP/Wide World Photos, p. 65 (bottom left); Chase Roe, Retna Ltd., p. 65 (bottom right); Jean Matheny, p. 66.